BUG BOOKS

Snail

Karen Hartley and Chris Macro

www.heinemann.co.uk/library
Visit our website to find out more information about Heinemann Library books.

To order:
 Phone 44 (0) 1865 888066
 Send a fax to 44 (0) 1865 314091
 Visit the Heinemann Bookshop at www.heinemann.co.uk/library to browse our catalogue and order online.

First published in Great Britain by Heinemann Library, Halley Court, Jordan Hill, Oxford OX2 8EJ, part of Harcourt Education.
Heinemann is a registered trademark of Harcourt Education Ltd.

Editorial: Clare Lewis and Katie Shepherd
Design: Ron Kamen, Michelle Lisseter and Bridge Creative Services Limited
Illustrations: Alan Male
Picture Research: Maria Joannou
Production: Helen McCreath

Printed and bound in China by South China Printers

10 digit ISBN 0 431 01835 9
13 digit ISBN 978 0 431 01835 5
10 09 08 07 06
10 9 8 7 6 5 4 3 2 1

British Library Cataloguing in Publication Data
Hartley, Karen
Bug Books: Snail - 2nd Edition
594.3
A full catalogue record for this book is available from the British Library.

Acknowledgements
The publishers would like to thank the following for permission to reproduce photographs:
Ardea London Ltd: pp14, 26, J Daniels p8, J Mason p13, P Morris p4; Bruce Coleman Ltd: J Burton pp24, 25, W Layer p23, H Reinhard p15, K Taylor pp11, 16, 20; FLPA: A Wharton p18; Chris Honeywell pp28, 29; Getty Images/The Image Bank: C Burki p22; Nature Photographers Ltd: P Sterry p12; Nature Picture Library: P Hobson p9; NHPA: M Tweedie p10; Oxford Scientific Films: G Bernard p27, L Crowhurst p7, W Gray p21, J Pontier p5; Planet Earth Pictures: S Hopkins pp6, 19; Premaphotos: K Preston-Mafham p17.

Cover photograph reproduced with permission of Ardea/Jean Michel Labat.

The publishers would like to thank Nancy Harris for her assistance in the preparation of this book.

Any words appearing in the text in bold, **like this**, are explained in the Glossary

Contents

What are snails?

Snails have a soft body and a hard shell. They do not have any legs. Some snails live in water. In this book we will look at snails that live in gardens and woods.

Snails come in different sizes and colours. Some snails are very small. Some are very big. This is a giant African land snail. It can grow to be longer than your foot!

soft foot

Snails have a thick, soft **foot** that they can pull into their hard shell. The soft foot usually feels damp and slimy.

Snails have four **feelers** on their heads. The short feelers are for touching and smelling. The long ones have two tiny eyes at the end.

long feelers

short feelers

How big are garden snails?

When it moves, an adult garden snail is nearly as long as your middle finger. Baby snails are about the size of your little fingernail.

Snails look much smaller when they are inside their shells. As snails grow, their shells get bigger.

How are snails born?

A snail makes a hole in the soil and
lays eggs there. The eggs are white.

eggs

After about 21 days, the eggs **hatch** and the baby snails begin to move about. They have small shells. Their bodies are very pale.

How do snails grow?

A snail's body gets darker as it gets older. It has rings on its shell. Each ring is called a **whorl**. In the first year the shell has about three whorls. Can you see them?

After two years, the snail is fully grown.
It has about five whorls on its shell.

What do snails eat?

Snails like to eat rotten leaves or plants. If there are no dead leaves, snails will eat fresh, green plants.

Algae is a green slime that grows on trees. Sometimes snails eat the algae. Some snails even eat other snails but they prefer to eat plants.

algae

Which animals attack snails?

Rats, large beetles and ducks like to eat snails. Some birds break open snail shells on a stone. The birds then eat the soft body inside.

When a snail thinks it is in danger it hides in its shell. Sometimes it makes bubbles called **froth** come out from under the shell. This scares off attackers.

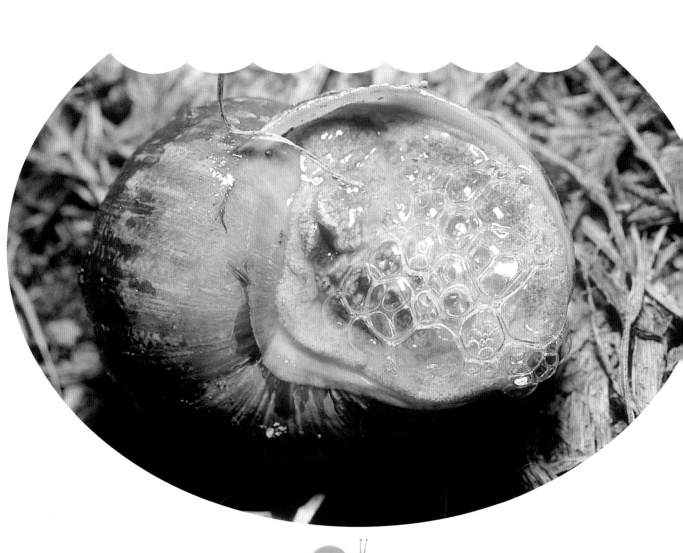

How do snails move?

Snails move slowly. They move quicker when it is warm and wet. The muscles in the **foot** make the snail move. Can you see the muscles in this foot?

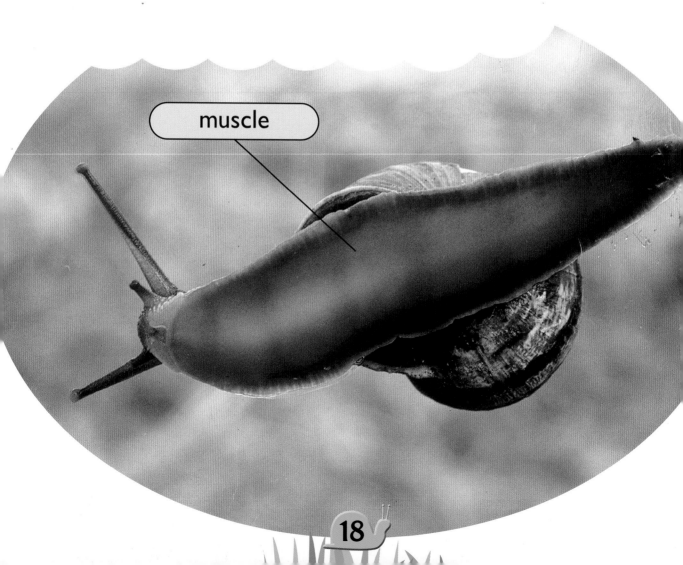

muscle

Snails make slime to help them slide over paths and stones. They make more slime when they are on slopes or rough ground.

Where do snails live?

Many snails live in gardens. They also live
in woods, hedges and in grass. They like
damp, dark places.

You can often find snails under stones.
After it has been raining you may see
them climbing up walls. Snails can cling
very tightly to walls and stones.

How long do snails live?

Garden snails can live for five years.
This is only if they stay safe from birds
and other enemies.

Some **desert** snails can live for much longer. They stay in their shells without eating or moving for many years.

What do snails do?

Snails come out when the weather is damp. When the weather is very hot snails stop eating and bury themselves. Snails also hide if the weather is very cold.

Snails look for food at night.
They are safer in the dark.

How are snails special?

Snails can smell strong smells with their **feelers**. If a snail smells something it does not like, it hides in its shell. Sometimes snails like to stay very close together.

Snails can make a skin over the opening of the shell. This is called the **epiphragm**. They make it when they go to sleep for the winter, or when it is hot.

epiphragm

Thinking about snails

Which food do you think the snail will like best? What are the snail's **feelers** used for?

Which surface is easier for the snail to move on? Will the snail make more slime when it is moving on the carpet or on the smooth wood?

Bug map

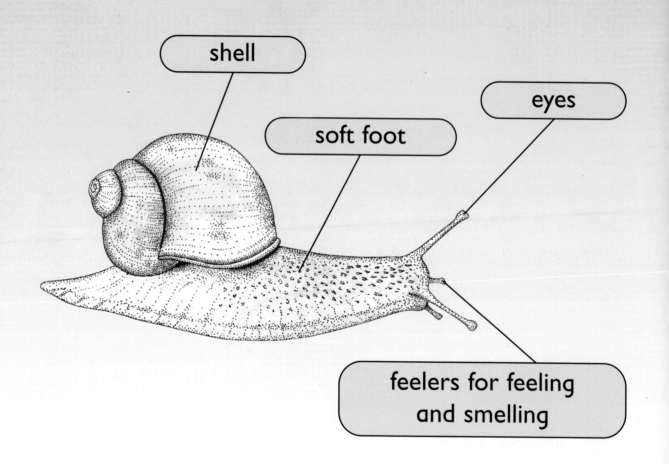

shell

soft foot

eyes

feelers for feeling and smelling

Actual size

Glossary

algae a green slime that grows on the branches and trunks of trees

desert bare land that has little or no rain

epiphragm the skin that the snail makes to cover the opening of its shell

feelers long thin tubes on a snail's head. These are used for feeling and smelling. The eyes are at the end of the long pair of feelers.

foot the soft body of the snail that comes out of the shell

froth a white foam that snails make when in danger. This comes out from under the shell.

hatch to come out of the egg

pale light in colour, almost white

whorls the rings on a snail's shell

Index

More books to read

Creepy Creatures: Snails, Monica Hughes
  (Heinemann Library, 2005)

Snails Up Close, Greg Pyers (Raintree, 2005)